# Breath of Steam

by
R. Keeley,
N. Preedy,
S. Wainwright.

Oxford Publishing Co

oPc

© Oxford Publishing Co. 1974

SBN 0 902888 37 4

Printed by B.H. Blackwell (Printing) Ltd.
in the City of Oxford

Photo reproduction and offset plates
by Oxford Litho Plates Ltd. Oxford.

Published by
Oxford Publishing Co.
5 Lewis Close
Risinghurst
Oxford, England.

# INTRODUCTION

Railway enthusiasts the world over enjoy watching the trains go by, and this enjoyment was always more intense if those trains happened to be hauled by a steam locomotive. After the primary satisfaction of just watching, came the secondary interest of documentation, and finally, if one was both fortunate and interested enough, came the joy of recording the passing railway scene, by means of camera and enlarger.

However, even when the subject was safely on negative, and a glossy print had been made, this was not the end, the ultimate satisfaction was achieved by showing off the results to other railway enthusiasts.

It was always necessary to be very diplomatic if one was chosen as a viewer. It could be that those shown were of top quality and really merited all the superlatives lavished upon them, but if, as so often was the case, that grey blur in one corner of the proffered picture was referred to as "the Cornish Riviera passing Dawlish Warren", it was vital to murmur words of wonderment and envy, or lose a friend for life!

However, amongst the thousands of rail enthusiasts, there are fortunately a handful of excellent photographers, who have travelled many miles about their particular locality, diligently putting on to film the railway scene of the past twenty years, recording in fact, the final act of the steam era.

The work of these stalwarts is really worth looking at but unfortunately, unless knowing each individual personally, and being invited to peruse each separate collection, many of us never have the privilege of inspecting the finished result of hours of travelling, scrambling, and waiting for that fleeting moment when the steam horse galloped by.

What a happy thought therefore, for three such railway photographers, to get together and each produce a cross section of his own collection, conjoin them all and, with the help of the Oxford Publishing Co, produce this delightful album of British Railway steam studies.

An old Chinese proverb quotes that "One picture tells more than a thousand words" which is very true no doubt, but a few words of explanation added to the illustration can often help in a greater appreciation of what lies hidden in the photograph.

This then is my humble contribution to this work. Whilst feeling rather inadequate for the task, I nevertheless feel it a great privilege, and drawing upon my years of professional railway experience, have tried to do justice to each and every photograph.

Realising only too well that it is the pictures that make this work, I have strived to keep the captions as short as possible, and yet still be at liberty to point out any item which has caught my notice. I am sure the reader will find much more in these studies than the words infer, but that is the attraction of looking at a set of new railway pictures.

I am sure that all readers will appreciate the labour of love and hard work that Raymond Keeley, Norman Preedy and Stanley Wainwright have put into these prints, to bring you "Breath of Steam".

*Jim Russell. 1974.*

1. What could be more fitting for a book of this title than this study of the streamlined class A4, No. 60024, *Kingfisher* at St. Margaret's Depot, Edinburgh. The date is 2nd September 1966 and although nearly at the end of the steam era, see how clean the engine and particularly the buffers are! This turntable was one of the many which were operated by the engine's own vacuum apparatus. Note the hose still connected at the rear, and the large reservoir at the right.

*Photo: Norman Preedy.*

2.  Those of us who have had the good fortune to visit an engine shed, can surely smell the steam in this shot of Darlington round house. The turntable occupied the centre and was open to the elements, with the engine stalls leading off in almost a complete circle. An interesting sample of tank engines are seen. From left to right: No. 68679 one of the 0-6-0T class of small shunter, designed by Worsdell in 1898, and classified J72. No. 69840 a large 4-6-2 tank class A5/2 built by Gresley in 1925 after a Robinson design. No. 68897 another Gresley, a smaller tank, 0-6-0T with 4' 8" driving wheels, class J50, and finally No. 69887 a 3 cylinder, 4-6-2T design which originated on the N.E. Railway in 1913. Classed as A8.

*Photo: R. Keeley.*

3.  A clear cold winter day in 1955, and the setting is Cheshire in the snow. No. 4683, one of the Collett 0-6-0 tanks, is acting as transfer pilot from the Midland region at Chester to Saltney yard. The long drag has just passed over the Junction points. Note the upper quadrant signals at the rear.

*Photo: S. D. Wainwright.*

4.  From Chester to the deep South! Three Southern region engines are seen here outside Fratton shed in June 1959. All three are in steam: No. 32646, the small Stroudley "Terrier" on the left, used for the Hayling Island Branch originally ex L.B.S.C., No. 30039 a Drummond 0-4-4T, which was built before the grouping for the L.S.W.R., and on the right, the 2-6-0 mixed traffic engine, 31809, a Southern Railway design by Maunsell. Note in the background the steam crane used for coaling some of the engines.

*Photo: R. Keeley.*

5.  The Massive Stanier Pacific class locomotive, No. 46209, *Princess Beatrice* pulls into Crewe station in August 1957, with the "Mid-Day Scot" from Euston. What large impressive engines these were, especially when seen like this, from a low viewpoint and head on. It is interesting to surmise the effect on Great Western Locomotive design, had William Stanier remained at Swindon, instead of transferring to the L.M.S.

*Photo: S. D. Wainwright*

6. In direct contrast to the previous express locomotive designed by W. Stanier, is this Fowler passenger engine of the 1930s. No. 45504 *Royal Signals* one of the "Patriot" class is seen at the head of a fitted freight train in the summer of 1955 running up the main line at Acton Bridge between Warrington and Crewe. Note the double arm signal on the left, in the off position, obviously like this for sighting purposes because of the over-bridge near to the station.

*Photo: S. D. Wainwright.*

7. A wisp of steam escapes from under No. 40094 as she starts away from Mobberley Station in May 1959. Mobberley was on the old Cheshire Lines Committee route from Manchester to Chester, but this train was for Crewe, via Northwich and Sandbach. Having five coaches, the train would probably have had to pull up in order to get all the vehicles to the small platform face.

*Photo: Norman Preedy.*

8. Still reasonably clean, after nearly fifty years' service, the ex L.N.W.R., Class G2, 0-8-0, heavy freight engine, trundles a long goods train past Acton Bridge in the summer of 1956. Originally built with round topped fireboxes, they were eventually fitted with the Belpaire type as seen here, and also lost their characteristic L.N.W. chimney. Note the loose three link coupling hanging on the front draw hook and the typical L.N.W.R. tender. As built, these engines were compounds, but rebuilt as "simples".

*Photo: S. D. Wainwright.*

9. Not the famous *King George V*, but her sister engine No. 6003 *King George IV* standing at the South end of Shrewsbury station awaiting the signal for "right away". The date of this picture is June 4th 1960 and only two years later she was to be found on the "withdrawn" sidings at Swindon!

*Photo: S. D. Wainwright.*

10. This picture shows the driver's side of No. 6003 and was taken on the same day and location as the previous photograph. The "King" class locomotives were only allowed North of Wolverhampton in the last few years of their life, the axle loading being too heavy in Great Western days for the Wolverhampton-Birkenhead line.

*Photo: S. D. Wainwright*

11. A study of Aintree shed in 1959. Many interesting engines could always be seen there. Even as late as May 1959, this picture shows No. 51537, on the left, one of the few survivors of the Aspinall designed 0-6-0Ts. Originally built in the 1897 period, this particular engine was the very last to go in 1961. The large 0-8-0 goods locomotive in the centre, No. 49668, is one of the Fowler freight engines built for the L.M.S. in the 1929-32 era. The tender and chimney are typically "Fowler" and being without vacuum brake apparatus, this engine was always on goods train duty.

*Photo: R. Keeley.*

12. A large engine with a small train. One of the Robinson Class 04, 2-8-0 freight engines is seen passing Northenden Junction in June 1957 with eight empty hoppers and a brake van! Northenden was another L.N.W. and C.L.C. junction just to the east of Altrincham and the west of Stockport. No. 63743 was one of the large class of ex-G.C. Railway designs which remained in the L.N.E.R. group. Others were used not only by the War Department, but by all other railway companies in Great Britain on return from military service.

*Photo: Norman Preedy.*

13. Saltney Junction, in November 1955, and one of the little Collett 0-4-2Ts of the Western Region, No. 1416, runs by the signal box *en route* to Oswestry from Chester. Her train consists of two of the "Thrush" type Auto trailers, perpetuating a system started in 1908 on the old Great Western.

*Photo: S. D. Wainwright.*

**14.** Oswestry on the 26th July 1960, showing the junction with the line to Gobowen. One of the Collett 2251 class of 0-6-0 engine comes off the branch, onto the old Cambrian main line. This small Shropshire town was once the headquarters of the Cambrian system which was primarily a Welsh railway, but all the locomotive servicing etc. was carried out in this north west corner of Salop. One unusual feature in this picture is the catch point bottom left, complete with moveable fouling bar, which had to follow the single throw-off blade.

*Photo: S. D. Wainwright.*

**15.** No. 7309 one of the Churchward 2-6-0 mixed traffic engines, built in 1921, pictured here with a Barmouth-Birkenhead train at Saltney Junction in June 1957. At this time the engine was in full passenger livery, with the "Lion" totem on the tender. She is carrying "stopping passenger" headlights as she had wandered across country from the Irish sea, but in fact was scheduled as a semi-fast. This Saltney Junction section was signalled, as can be seen, with Midland Region equipment.

*Photo: S. D. Wainwright.*

16.    A white feather of steam from the Stanier Jubilee *Aboukir* No. 45681, as she breaks through that low parapet of Acton Bridge station. The long slanting March sunlight of 1957, lights up the driver's side as she takes the Liverpool boat train up the West Coast Main Line. I like that oil lamp still in use on the bridge on the right and the old "Midland" van on the left.

*Photo: Norman Preedy.*

17.    Built in 1938, this massive engine *Coronation* No. 46220 was the first of Stanier's enlarged "Princess" class. Originally known as the Princess Coronation series they were eventually merged into the "Duchess" class, and were among the largest engines to run on the Midland region metals. Seen in this picture with the cylinder cocks open, she prepares to leave Chester station. The train is the 12.50 p.m. Bangor-Euston express photographed in August 1961.

*Photo: S. D. Wainwright.*

18. Just arrived at King's Cross, this famous engine, *Flying Scotsman*, little knew what fate had in store for her! This picture was taken in October 1959 and shows the ugly double chimney and the B.R. number 60103. When finally retired, she was purchased by Alan Pegler who restored her to her former L.N.E.R. glory with original livery, chimney and number 4472. She then set out on many journeys for enthusiasts, culminating in a trip across the Atlantic, where she was nearly lost for good, but fortunately she was purchased by a well known enthusiast and brought back to Britain and restored once again for the delight of all steam enthusiasts.

*Photo: R. Keeley.*

19. Another Jubilee class, this time No. 45703 *Thunderer* heading towards Crewe with a Bangor-Euston express in August 1955 east of Waverton station, having passed over water troughs and through Christleton tunnel.

*Photo: S. D. Wainwright.*

**20.**

The south end of Shrewsbury station, on the 30th May 1958 and the fireman of No. 7023 *Penrice Castle* awaits the "right away" signal from the train guard, before telling his driver to proceed towards Hereford with a Welsh express.

*Photo: S. D. Wainwright.*

**21.**

One can always distinguish a rail-tour special from the lineside, not only by the head-boards which proclaim the venue, but from the numerous heads looking out of every available window. This "Jubilee", No. 45705 *Seahorse* has just left Cheadle Heath Junction on the old Midland line near Stockport, and is heading for the High Peak district. From the black smoke, it would appear that the fire has just been charged ready for work on the bank. Note the three types of track, chaired on the left, concrete sleepers in the centre, and flat bottomed spiked under the train.

*Photo: Norman Preedy.*

**22.** There is no steam being used on the "Battle of Britain" class, 4-6-2 No. 34068 *Kenley*, as she descends the final stretch with the Dover Boat Train in August 1952. This short distance between Folkestone and Dover was an expensive section of railway threading its way along the sea-shore under the chalk cliffs, and through the three tunnels. However, the heavy Continental traffic soon repaid the capital outlay. How strange that the Southern Region, the first to use main line electrification, was the last to retain steam working.

*Photo: Norman Preedy.*

**23.** On the 29th Sept. 1962 at Ruabon, "Hall" class, No. 6915 *Mursley Hall* runs into the station with a Shrewsbury-Chester express. Not only has this train "clear" signals, but there is also "line clear" on the "up" road as one can see from the "Starter" and "Distant" in the "off" position beyond the signal box. The A.T.C. ramp in the foreground, is for that same distant signal and would at that moment in time be electrified. This would give a clear signal in the cab of the next engine to pass over it (if ex-G.W.R.).

*Photo: S. D. Wainwright.*

24. I was always fascinated by these tiny Stroudley "Terriers" and having had the pleasure of sailing at Hayling Island, I came to know them well. They were long lived, being built as far back as 1880, and how odd they looked coupled to the large Southern region stock. This picture shows No. 32677, standing at Hayling Island Station in June of 1959 ready to depart for Havant. I was told that the spark arrester was a precaution against setting fire to the wooden viaduct bridge which these trains had to cross to gain the mainland. For those interested, No. 32677, was built in 1880 for the L.B.S.C. Railway as No. 77 and named *Wonersh*. Retired by the Southern Railway in 1925 and stored, she did a spell on the Isle of Wight from 1927 and returned to Eastleigh under British Rail in 1949.

*Photo: R. Keeley.*

25. A study which illustrates Chester General "train shed" roof, already mentioned. There was something of everything at Chester, a terminus, a triangle, long platform faces, and even through roads. In the early days many railway companies' engines and stock could be seen here, rather like a North Western "York". This picture taken on July 18th 1959 shows a relief train to the "up" Irish mail passing on the "through" road, and with a very interesting engine at the head. This is No. 45500, *Patriot*, the first of her class. She was rebuilt to this design by Fowler from the original "Claughton", and with her sister engine No. 5501 retained the special "Claughton" driving wheels, which can clearly be seen in this picture. Note the large heavy centre bosses.

*Photo: S. D. Wainwright.*

26. Two specially cleaned and prepared "Western" engines shown at Ruabon on 29th September 1962. They were to work the annual members' train to Towyn for the A.G.M. of the Talyllyn Railway Preservation Society. As a founder member of the T.R.P.S. it was always a delight to see this special train from Paddington, packed with devotees, making the beautiful cross-country journey to the Merioneth coast. Engines had to change at Ruabon, as only light axle loading locomotives were allowed over the Cambrian section; hence No. 7801 and No. 7314 standing ready at Ruabon on the goods loop.

*Photo: S. D. Wainwright.*

27. The 3.45 p.m. Oswestry to Gobowen local starts out from the bay at the Cambrian head-quarters after making connection with the train from Aberystwyth. The date is July 1960, and with the two passenger trains and the goods in the platform road the photo captures a scene of great activity. The goods shed is seen on the right, the old Cambrian offices can be spotted over and to the left of the gantry, and the carriage sidings on the left behind the steam of No. 1458. Note the train formation, one Brake-Compo and an Auto-trailer car.

*Photo: S. D. Wainwright.*

28. Salop shed will always be remembered for their clean engines, and No. 7023 *Penrice Castle* pictured here, is a shining example of their work and care. She is standing in No. 7 platform at Shrewsbury station at the head of a Manchester-Plymouth express with a full head of steam in 1958. The engine has obviously just backed on to the train, as both guard and engineman are checking the connection between engine and coach.

*Photo: S. D. Wainwright.*

29. This scene shows the Aberystwyth-Crewe train, leaving Oswestry station heading towards Whitchurch and eventually Crewe. The engine is *Foxcote Manor*, No. 7822, and one of the series with the peculiar waisted chimney. Note that the goods train, which was standing at the other platform, has been put away, and the engine is backing down, prior to dropping on to the shed.

*Photo: S. D. Wainwright.*

30. One of the A.1 class Pacific locomotives of Peppercorn design built for the old L.N.E.R. just before nationalization, seen at Waverley Edinburgh, already prepared for the next duty. Waverley Box can be seen top right, with the catwalk just over the tender top. Note the "belt and braces" headlamps. Although fitted with electric lamps, No. 60161 still sticks to the oil lamp on the smoke box indicating light engine! What handsome locomotives, these three cylinder Pacifics were, several of which were named after the constituent companies i.e. *Great Central*, and the *North British* illustrated on this page.

*Photo: Norman Preedy.*

31. One of the first 28XX series of the old Great Western No. 2802 (rebuilt of course), but very much as she was built in 1905, is seen here in August 1955 dragging a long freight train up Gresford bank, heading south towards Wrexham. Carrying "F" headlights and nearly fifty years old, the engine still has a powerful exhaust, one can almost hear her pounding up the gradient!

*Photo: S. D. Wainwright.*

32. "D" headlights on this A.3 at Newcastle on Tyne denote that this train is a fast-fitted freight. No. 60071 *Tranquil*, one of the Gresley Pacifics of the same design as *Flying Scotsman*, is seen here pulling a freight train through Central station with traffic for the East Coast. Note the engine has the early L.N.E.R. tender with rails, and the experimental German smoke deflectors.

*Photo: Norman Preedy.*

33. A comparison of style in mixed traffic engines. On the right two Stanier class 5s are seen heading the Manchester-Llandudno express into Chester General station in June 1962, whilst standing at the old L.N.W.R. bracket signal, is one of the "Modified" Hall class of the Western region. This engine is *Fountains Hall* and was built in 1949 for British Railways, but is still pure Great Western in appearance. Nevertheless the two classes have much in common, note the plate frames, outside steam pipes, Belpaire fireboxes etc.

*Photo: S. D. Wainwright.*

34. One of four engines built to this class, No. 30494 is of the unusual wheel arrangement 4-8-0T. This quartet was originally built by the L.S.W. Railway to a design by the then C.M.E., Robert W. Urie, for work in the newly constructed hump yard at Feltham in 1921. Classified by the L.S.W.R. as G16, the four engines were virtually unchanged throughout their life. They were heavy engines, being 95 tons in working order, and with a width of 9' 2", were one of the widest locos at work in the country. Not handsome maybe, but with a look of power about her, No. 30494 is shown at Feltham in 1959. Note the smokebox door uncleated, perhaps for tube cleaning.

*Photo: R. Keeley.*

35. This class of 2-6-0 moguls were always known to railwaymen and enthusiasts alike as "Crabs", perhaps on account of those large inclined cylinders in front and that massive motion bracket? But their history goes back to the time when George Hughes of the L. & Y. Railway Company became C.M.E. of the L.M.S. in 1922 after the grouping. At that time a general purpose locomotive was needed, and so this small-wheeled 2-6-0 was designed and built. No. 42705 is seen at Newton Heath in 1958.

*Photo: R. Keeley.*

36. Nostalgic memories of holidays spent at Dawlish, what a wonderful spot for railway enthusiasts! Lovely sands for the children and wives, and a continuous stream of Swindon engines sweeping past under the red sandstone for the delight of the fathers. Even in B.R. days, they were still "Western" trains, and this picture of No. 6008 *King James II* at the east end of the station with the Paddington bound "Mayflower" portrays this.

*Photo: Norman Preedy.*

37. A Black "5" at Bangor in 1965. In the picture one can see the water column with its extended pipe, the bracket signal with the two arms for the Junction just the other side of the tunnel, and the Bangor box, built into the retaining wall of the cutting. The entrance to Bangor tunnel can just be seen beyond and to the left of the lattice signal post.

*Photo: S. D. Wainwright.*

38.  The approach tracks to Crewe station from the North as seen in 1953. The Stanier Jubilee No. 45566 *Queensland* runs into the Junction, with a fourteen coach train from Bangor. Another Euston bound train from the North can be seen approaching over the Manchester line Junction. The longest platform at Crewe can just be seen on the centre right, always a favourite site for spotters and photographers.

*Photo: S. D. Wainwright.*

39.  One of the large four cylinder "Princess" class, No. 46207, is seen here entering Crewe from the south, the opposite end of the station to that of the picture above. This engine was named *Princess Arthur of Connaught* and I could never fathom this mix-up in gender!

*Photo: S. D. Wainwright.*

40.  Saltney Junction again, but this time a North British built 2-8-0 freight engine No. 90392 with a heavy train of loaded hoppers bound for Mold Junction. The class was designed by R. A. Riddles in 1943 for use on military service during the Second World War. No less than 733 were returned to British Railways after hostilities ceased, and served all over the United Kingdom.

*Photo: S. D. Wainwright.*

41.    Steam on the electric lines! A rather scruffy rebuilt West Country Class No. 34036 *Westward Ho* stands at the platform edge at Basingstoke in 1966. Like the "Princess" class on the Midland Region, these Southern engines were built to the limit of the height of the loading gauge laid down by Bulleid, and the first batch were streamlined. They had many defects when built as indeed does any unorthodox design, but with the casing removed and conventional valve gear replacing the original, these machines did excellent work, especially over the hilly Somerset and Dorset route. For the record, the train shown in this photograph is a Weymouth-Waterloo express.

*Photo: Norman Preedy.*

42.    Swindon General in the Spring of 1962, and No. 7035 *Ogmore Castle* starts to pick up speed again after coming off the curve and over the junction at the west end of the station. The train is the "Cheltenham Spa Express" which used to be known as the "Flyer" but only from Swindon. The timing was very easy until reaching here, and then a mad dash was made for Paddington, resulting in the service being known for many years as "The World's Fastest Train"!

*Photo: Norman Preedy.*

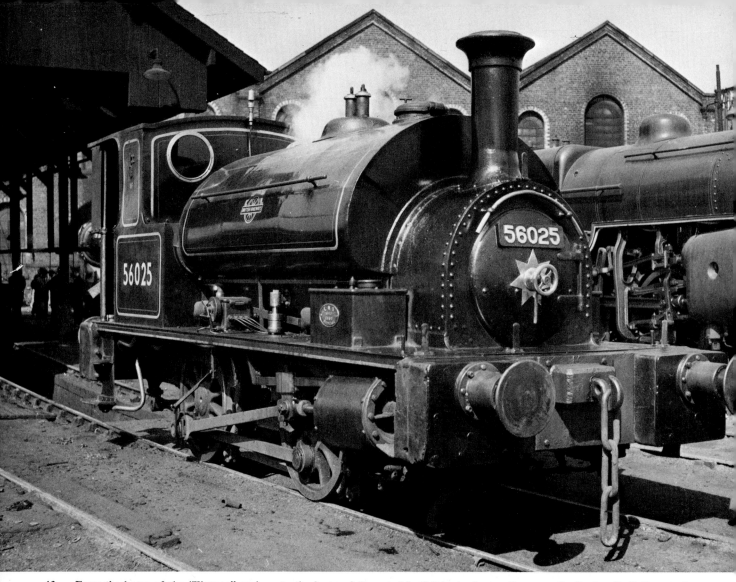

43. From the home of the "Western" engines, to the home of the erstwhile Caledonian locomotives over the Border. St. Rollux, to the North of Glasgow, is the setting for this little "Pug" 0-4-0T, looking very well cared for after fifty years' service.

First built between 1878 and 1908, they were a pure Caledonian design by Dugald Drummond, and have been passed on down to the L.M.S. and finally to the Scottish Region of British Railways. When pictured in May 1957, she looked as if she could carry on for many more years. Notice the typical "Caley" star on the smokebox door! Tradition dies hard, thank goodness!!

*Photo: R. Keeley.*

44. A study of a Stanier "Black 8", one of the many hundreds of 8F freight engines, designed by William Stanier in 1935, primarily for the old L.M.S.R. but eventually seeing service overseas with the War Department. These engines were built at Crewe, Swindon, Doncaster, Ashford, Darlington, Eastleigh and Brighton. The example illustrated here is No. 48630 at the head of an Irish cattle special, gliding through the network of points at Chester General in September of 1962.

*Photo: S. D. Wainwright.*

45. Two "light axle" engines at Machynellth Shed in August 1959. This far flung locomotive depot was a three road shed, and when built had to be blasted out of the rock cutting on one side of the track. The other side of the running line was Corris station. The two engines seen in this shot are, on the right, one of the last series of small-wheeled Prairie tanks of the 55XX class, and on the left a Dukedog Class No. 9017 which is a combination of the Duke and Bulldog classes. No. 9017 was purchased by the Bluebell line, and has been restored and renumbered 3217.

*Photo: Norman Preedy.*

46. No. 9017 again, and this time wearing "A" headlamps indicating *Express passenger*. This was in August 1960 and shows the little "Dukedog" acting as pilot and banker for the "Cambrian Coast Express". The train has just pulled into Shrewsbury station and 9017 has backed on, and will assist No. 7818 *Granville Manor* across the old Cambrian route to the coast. Note the L.N.W.R. signals amongst the girders of Shrewsbury station.

*Photo: S. D. Wainwright.*

47.  In 1957 *City of Truro*, the famous little Great Western engine whose reputed 103 mph in 1904 earned her a place in York Museum, came out of honourable retirement, was repainted and checked over at Swindon and proceeded to delight fans all over the country by working rail tours. This picture shows No. 3440 at Ruabon in March of 1957, whilst at the head of one of the specials. She was painted in the old 1900 livery of Indian red and green and looked superb. What a pity Swindon Museum repainted her again in green and black!

*Photo: S. D. Wainwright.*

48.  More than a breath of steam here! *Sir Vincent Raven*, No. 60126, starts away on a vicious curve from West Hartlepool Station during August 1960. This 3 cylinder Pacific was another of the Peppercorn "A1" Class. When first built she was painted in the lovely L.N.E.R. apple green with black and white lining, but in the photograph No. 60126 is wearing the standard B. R. green, with black and orange lining. The train she is hauling is the York-Newcastle express working via the East Coast Route from Darlington via Hartlepools and Sunderland, composed of L.N.E.R. stock.

*Photo: Norman Preedy.*

9. A Thompson and a Gresley design, stand side by side at Sheffield Victoria in July 1958; steam under the electric catenaries! No. 61380, one of the Thompson B.1s which was a very useful 2 cylinder general purpose engine built between 1942 and 1950, stands at the platform face with the 3.10 p.m. Sheffield-Marylebone. The "Sandringham" class B.17 designed by Gresley with 3 cylinders, waits on the middle road.

*Photo: R. Keeley.*

50. A British Railway's "Britannia" class enters Chester General station with the up "Welshman" in August 1963. These engines were designed by the Railway Executive Engineers, gathered together under the direction of Mr. R.A. Riddles on the formation of British Railways as a National undertaking. The engines were classed as 7 M.T. "Pacific" and, as the first machine was named *Britannia*, so the class as a series kept this title. They had a very short history, as the diesel-electric traction started to supersede them in 1958. This particular example is No. 70054 *Dornoch Firth*.

*Photo: S. D. Wainwright.*

51. Another comparison page! Two 4-6-0s of different ancestry, and yet linked by the Swindon locomotive factory. No. 6945 *Glasfryn Hall* was built by the G.W.R. in 1942, whereas No. 46154 is one of the "Royal Scot" class built by the old L.M.S.R. William Stanier, who served his apprenticeship at Swindon, rose to be second in command under Collett, until 1932 when he left the G.W.R. and became Chief Mechanical Engineer of the L.M.S.R. at Crewe.

So, backing on to the shed at Chester, are two engines, one directly descended from a Churchward design, and the other complete with smoke deflectors, showing the same Swindon locomotive practices and design.
*Photo: S. D. Wainwright.*

52. The parcels service consisted of many types of vans of all regions, and conveyed the large volume of passenger parcels traffic at express speed, over and above the small amount which travelled in the passenger train guard's van. This picture shows a parcels train carrying "D" headlights. This old rebuilt "Star" Class, No. 4061 *Glastonbury Abbey*, is seen passing Saltney Junction in 1954, with one of the northbound "Parcels". These trains were also used to move rolling stock from point to point about the system, so saving delays to ordinary passenger trains.
*Photo: S. D. Wainwright.*

53. Three years after nationalization, in 1951, No. 46163 *Civil Service Rifleman* is pictured entering Crewe station with a 13 coach express from Euston. The engine is one of the "Royal Scot" Class, which were built in 1927-30, for the L.M.S.R. to Henry Fowler's design. They were the class which carried the brunt of the express passenger work on that system until Mr. Stanier's designs and rebuilds started to ease the load. This "Scot" Class was one which was later transformed with a taper boiler, new cylinders, new bogies, Swindon pattern axleboxes and springs, and the G.W.R. pattern of smokebox saddle, cast with the inside cylinder. In fact, all that was used of the original engines were the wheels, frames and motion! Note that No. 46163 has the British Railways lettering on the tender, soon superseded by the small "Lion".

*Photo: S. D. Wainwright.*

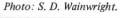

54. This book not only shows examples of steam in B.R. days, but also many engines of the old constituent companies. This sunny picture was taken inside old "New Street" station Birmingham on the occasion of a Stephenson Locomotive Society's run to Doncaster. It shows the superb paintwork and finish on No. 1000, the preserved Deeley Compound, which was brought out of Derby for this special trip in August 1959. Of course the photograph should have been in colour, to get the impact of that lovely Midland red with the straw lining and post box red buffer beam. I remember this occasion so well; this beautiful machine shone out in the murk of New Street like a butterfly on a slag bank! However sad to relate, her performance on this trip, was not very sparkling, but it was a joy to see her in action again.

*Photo: Norman Preedy.*

55. Railwaymen always liked having their photographs taken, they were proud of their job, and of the steam engines they worked with. This self-conscious group, is the staff concerned with the rather sad last day of the Oldham, Ashton and Guide Bridge service, plus of course the Robinson 4-4-2T, class C13 and one coach which worked over the branch. One odd fact about this line which connected Guide Bridge with Oldham via Ashton, was that it retained its independence until 1948, and even on the 2nd May 1959 (the date of this photograph) tickets were still issued bearing the O.A. and G.B. initials!

*Photo: R. Keeley*

57. Another large engine with a small train No. 49404, one of the old L.N.W.R. "Super D's", trundles past Waverton down home signal in 1954 with eight wagons and van. These engines started life from a Webb 3-cylinder design of compound 0-8-0 coal engine, gradually changing to a 2-cylinder simple with a large boiler, and eight-coupled small size driving wheels. The rebuild was to drawings by Whale, and the classification then given as Class "D". In 1912, superheaters were added to this class, and so, from here on, these heavy freight engines became known as the "Super D's" although the class name in the official books was "G1", later made "G2" when a higher boiler pressure was used.

*Photo: S. D. Wainwright.*

56. Dropping down through Ruabon station heading towards Shrewsbury on a July day in 1952, is No. 2864, one of the ex-Great Western Railway's heavy 2-8-0 engines, on an "H" headlight "Through goods to destination" train. Of Churchward design, one of these engines took part in the locomotive exchanges in 1921, being sent to Scotland to work on the Glenfarg bank. However, meeting a snowstorm, she got her sandpipes choked and slipped to a standstill, which was most unusual for "Western" engines. Later in 1948 the class took part in the 1948 exchanges working on the Southern, Eastern and Midland Regions, and showed very free steaming, with the regulator, but considerable fore and aft oscillation.

The lattice work girder in the picture is the footbridge joining the two platforms, and replaced the old wooden gabled type which used to suffice, but which was prone to fire hazards.

*Photo: Norman Preedy.*

58. A "Midland" locomotive passing a "Midland" signal box on "Midland" metals in 1959. Class "4F" No. 44556, one of the 772 engines originally built in 1911 to this 0-6-0 design by Fowler for the old Midland Railway. It is seen here approaching Gowhole sidings on the main line, and is just passing over the crossover, which connects the main line to the slow lines. Note the long check rail alongside the inner running rail.

*Photo: R. Keeley.*

59. Another of the snow scenes of 1955 captured by Mr. Wainwright's camera. The location is again Saltney Junction and the dark train contrasts sharply with the white surroundings. One redeeming feature of snow to the railway photographer is that it does tend to reflect light up on to the darker parts of locomotives, and so it is with this ex-L.M.S., 2-6-0 Stanier design of 1933, No. 42971. Notice the reflected light on the wheels, cylinders and motion. Cold feet were a small price to pay for this good shot.

*Photo: S. D. Wainwright.*

60. "Castle" Class No. 5070, *Sir Daniel Gooch* sets off from Wrexham in August 1961 with the 4.30 p.m. Birkenhead-Paddington express, having just passed over the Croes Newydd North Junction. Shedded at Stafford Road, No. 5070 is a credit to the cleaners there, spotlessly clean, with all her brass and copperwork shining, and with all her piston glands steam tight. Named after one of the illustrious Great Western Engineers, she was one of three "Castles" to be so honoured, the other two being No. 5069 *Isambard Kingdom Brunel* and No. 7017 *G. J. Churchward.*

*Photo: S. D. Wainwright.*

61. A case of the "early bird catching the worm". R. Keeley's fine shot of these two Fowler Class "3F's", Nos. 43715 & 43243, pulling away from Cheadle Heath with a long train, was caught at 7.50 a.m. on the 12th April 1958. It is an unusual picture too, as the motive power rostered for this goods train was one of the Stanier "Black 8s", so it was a lucky break to get this action picture of the pair of 0-6-0s blasting their way out of the station yard. Obviously they had waited their turn, until the Buxton-Manchester business train had entered the platform road.

*Photo: R. Keeley.*

62. Rail and road as a very small 0-4-0 saddle tank ventures forth onto the streets of Manchester from Salford Goods Yard in September 1959. This little engine (she was indeed small, compare her with the box van astern) was one of a series of dock tanks designed by Aspinall and built for the L. and Y. Railway between 1891 and 1910. Taken over by the L.M.S., twenty-three came into B.R. service, and some even lasted into the "sixties". Note the dumb buffers and enclosed crossheads.

*Photo: R. Keeley.*

63. On the 29th September 1962, the Talyllyn Railway Preservation Society members were lucky enough to secure the services of No. 6000 *King George V* herself to haul their A.G.M. special from Paddington, and in this picture she is seen, just having come off the train at Ruabon and dropping back "bunker first" to Salop shed for light refreshment!

As remarked previously the "King" class of locomotive in Great Western days was classified as "Double Red", which meant their axle loading was too heavy for work North of Stafford Road, Wolverhampton. But, here we see her not far from Chester, obviously those weak bridges and viaducts must have been strengthened in B.R. days! However, even with British Railways, she was far too large for working over the branch line from Ruabon, and so the "Z85" special went on from here, with two lighter engines.

*Photo: S. D. Wainwright.*

**64.** Time passes, and engines get bigger, and trains smaller! This picture taken from an overbridge looks down on one of the Hawksworth "County Class" with a four coach express from Leamington to Birkenhead. The location is again Saltney Junction, a favourite spot for Mr. Wainwright, and on this fine August day in 1962 he has captured nicely not only the double chimneyed No. 1026, *County of Salop*, but also given us a good idea of the track layout at this approach to Chester. Note the different heights of the upper quadrant signals, one on a tubular post, and the other on the old L.N.W.R. wooden type.

*Photo: S. D. Wainwright.*

**65.** Taken from the same fine viewpoint as before, but this time in 1952, this scene includes another "Down" train with a 25 wagon goods train in charge, a "5IXX" class 2-6-2 tank. These big "Prairie" tanks were allocated and used all over the Western Region, working passenger suburbans around Paddington, Birmingham, Cardiff and Bristol, and, as can be seen here, were just as happy working a goods train backwards, as they were pulling fast trains forward!

*Photo: S. D. Wainwright.*

66. Each railway photographer has several favourite lineside spots, and this is very evident in this book. Norman Preedy had one such spot on the railway bank just outside West Hartlepool station, and from this site took this action picture of No. 60073, ex-L.N.E.R., Class A3 locomotive, *St. Gatien.*

The date was August 1960 and the big Pacific is pulling off the station curve, with a Kings Cross-Newcastle express via the East Coast route, from Darlington. Seen over the engine's boiler, is one of the timber yards that abound around here, for the Baltic timber which is shipped to the port. To the right of the yard, a train of hopper empties, awaits the departure of the express before proceeding on her own way.

*Photo: Norman Preedy.*

67. Another shot of No. 6000, *King George V*, this time at the head of the scheduled "Cambrian Coast Express" on 5th August 1960. She has just worked this train down from Paddington (via Bicester) and would no doubt come off here at Shrewsbury, to be turned for the return to London with an "Up" express. Note the severe curve here at the South end of Shrewsbury station, and the tall L.N.W.R. signal box in the rear.

*Photo: S. D. Wainwright.*

**68.** Bolton (Trinity Street), and in the carriage sidings stands the last survivor of many 2-4-2Ts built originally to designs of Aspinall for the old L. and Y. Railway. The date of the photograph is 3rd April 1959, seventy years after building of this class commenced. This 2-4-2 tank type was the first engine class to be built at Horwich works. In their day they were remarkable little engines shuttling in and out of Manchester with 10 suburban carriages, and keeping time day after day with startling regularity. All in all 330 were built, and of course were absorbed by the L.M.S.R., and eventually quite a few served under British Rail ownership.

*Photo: R. Keeley.*

**69.** Shrewsbury station in June 1960 and No. 6025, *King Henry III,* has just arrived with the "Cambrian Coast Express".

*Photo: S. D. Wainwright.*

70. One of the North British Locomotive Company's big Austerity 2-8-0 freight engines shoving hard at the rear of a goods train through Davenport station on the Buxton branch. A tender full of dirty coal has no doubt created all that black smoke, and although very nice for the photographer it is hardly appreciated by the passengers resting under the station verandah! The number of the engine was 90642.

*Photo: R. Keeley.*

71. Gresford Bank, on the line between Wrexham and Saltney, was one of Mr. Wainwright's photographic sites, and in the autumn of 1955, this train of empty stock was caught climbing the gradient with No. 6980, *Llanrumney Hall* at the head. It is interesting to compare this shot, with a similar one in plate 31, taken in the summer of the same year. In the interim, the long siding on the right has been lifted completely, and the sleepers and rails await the Sunday P.W. train for removal. The grade can be assessed by the plane of the siding which was practically level.

*Photo: S. D. Wainwright.*

**72.** A superb portrait of another rebuilt "Battle of Britain" Class Pacific. *Lord Dowding*, No. 34052, sets off from Basingstoke station on the 20th May 1966 heading a Waterloo-Weymouth express. This engine started life with the air smoothing casing, but later had it removed together with the chain valve gear, and, as can be seen here a very workmanlike engine ensued. I particularly like the lattice post signals on the gantry, a purely L.S.W. Railway practice. One can spot these pregrouping features cropping up in dozens of rail pictures.

*Photo: Norman Preedy.*

73.   An ex-G.W.R. "Castle" figures in this photograph, steaming freely with a Leamington-Birkenhead express at Saltney Junction again. The engine is No. 5097 *Sarum Castle* built in 1939 and still looking good in 1957, coupled to a Hawksworth 4000 gallon slab-sided tender. The high overbridge behind the steam is the very same that Mr. Wainwright used as a high viewpoint for the pictures in plates 64 and 65.

*Photo: S. D. Wainwright.*

74.   No. 7015 *Carn Brea Castle* was one of the first of the "Castle" Class to be built at Swindon under the aegis of British Railways in 1948. She is seen here at Chester in May 1962 wearing "B" headlamps and preparing to take out the 2.45 p.m. Birkenhead-Paddington train (the headcode was changed to "A" just before departure). Note the double chimney, which I could never admire on the "Castles", and the shed code "89A" an innovation of British Railways. The guard is seen giving the driver the train compilation and loading.

*Photo: S. D. Wainwright.*

**75.** Leeds City Station in May 1958 and the Gresley Pacific *Gainsborough* stands at the head of a Leeds-Glasgow express which was called "The North Briton", leaving at 9.05 a.m. Being of the same lineage as the "Flying Scotsman" they started off as G.N. Railway 4-6-2s with a boiler pressure of 180 lbs at which time they were classed as "A1", but upon being fitted with new boilers pressed at 220 lbs, they were upgraded to "A3". On the left inside the station can be seen a class "B1" on a train of empty stock.

*Photo: R. Keeley.*

**76.** This ex-Great Central design is *Princess Mary*, No. 62664, one of the enlarged "Director" Class. The first batch of "Directors" (so called because some were named after the directors of the old G.C. Railway) were built to a Robinson design in 1913 and classed "D10". Later in 1920-22 a further eleven engines were constructed which were slightly larger, with double window cab, and other modifications. These were classed "DII/I" and called enlarged "Directors". Our picture was taken at Woodhouse in July 1968, when she was working a Retford-Sheffield train.

*Photo: R. Keeley.*

77. This full frontal view of Britannia Class, No. 70038, *Robin Hood* really shows what large engines these British Railway 2 cylinder-Pacifics were. Taken at Leeds City Station on July 21st 1967, she was acting as the train engine on a Stephenson Locomotive Society's special, running from York to Birmingham.

*Photo: Norman Preedy.*

78. Sunlight and shadow at Croes Newydd in June 1959. One of the "Churchward" moguls, No. 6357 stands outside the shed with a full head of steam, as can be seen by the steam gauge in the cab, but correctly left in mid gear for safety's sake. Many questions have been asked about these engines as to the possibility of any of them being lined out. This picture dispels any doubt about No. 6357, as the B.R. lining can clearly be seen on both tender and cab side. For the record, Croes Newydd shed was to the south of Wrexham, and situated in the Minera Branch triangle.

*Photo: S. D. Wainwright.*

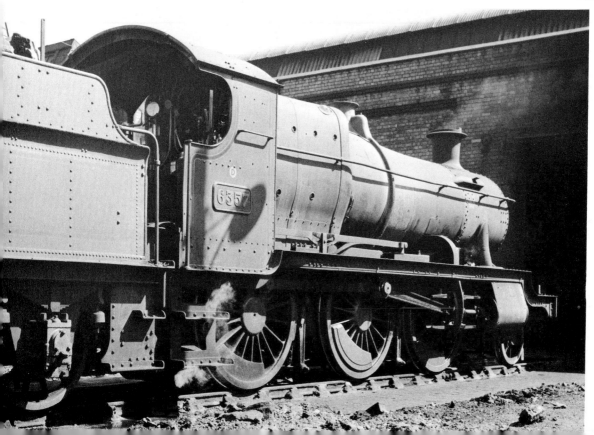

79. What at first sight could be Dawlish in Devon, is in fact South of New Mills Station in Derbyshire, and the train is a Manchester-Chinley local passenger. The engine is one of the British Railways Class "5s" which were produced by Mr. Riddles and his staff as a lighter version of the "Britannias". In fact these "Mixed Traffic" 4-6-0s were very akin to a scaled down "Britannia", many of the boiler and motion features being of very similar style to their larger sisters.

*Photo: R. Keeley.*

80. On May 11th 1963 in exactly the same location as that in plate 74 (Chester General) is a very different engine, No. 1000, the final development of the 2 cylinder Great Western "Saint" Class. Designed by Mr. Hawksworth in 1945, No. 1000 was unnamed at first, and was the only engine to carry the special copper-topped double chimney. Straight name plates were later added bearing the name *County of Middlesex*.

*Photo: S. D. Wainwright.*

81. Another picture of *City of Truro* at Ruabon in March 1957, for the working of the Festiniog Railway Society's special train, carrying the Society's headboard, with the emblem of the Prince of Wales feathers. What a picture she made, all spit and polish! I well remember when this little engine came back from the Scottish Exhibition, she passed outside my house, and the friendly signalman stopped her for my benefit so that I could photograph her colourful livery. Alas, nowadays, No. 3440 is static in Swindon museum.

*Photo: S. D. Wainwright.*

82. Shades of things to come! Stanier Pacific No. 46209 *Princess Beatrice* stands at the south end of Crewe station in July 1959, underneath the unfinished electric catenary gantries. As soon as the cables were installed and the electric trains rolling, so the "Lizzies", as the "Princess Class" were known, gradually faded away and vanished.

*Photo: Norman Preedy.*

83. A photograph taken in August 1961 by Mr. Wainwright, but, with the exception of that double chimney, it could so easily be the Great Western Railway scene of 1939! A Collett "Castle" No. 5095, *Barbury Castle* built in 1939 passes Croes Newydd with a Bournemouth-Birkenhead cross-country express. This train ran, one in each direction, each day in the thirties, and those wooden posted signals with their wooden arms are pure Great Western, even the water column, supplying both main line and loop line, is a Swindon product.         *Photo: S. D. Wainwright.*

84.

Mention has been made previously of the "Royal Scott" class, which H. G. Ivatt rebuilt for the L.M.S., and made into such excellent free-running engines. Here is another example of the "Rebuilt Scot" Class, No. 46165, *The Ranger 12th London Regiment*. Fitted with smoke deflectors and painted B.R. green she is seen between Chester and Waverton in September 1956 with the 12.50 p.m. Bangor to Euston express. Coaches at that time were painted strawberry and cream, not a happy colour combination, and I feel they looked much better in the Midland Lake.

*Photo: S. D. Wainwright.*

85. There is a story in this picture of Chester station on the 7th October 1961, with *City of Lancaster* standing at the platform. Suddenly, along drifts an unmanned ex-G.W. "7341", having run away from the shed. Fortunately, she was boarded and stopped in the station just after this picture was taken. If the reversing lever had been put amidships as in the photo on page 78, this could never have happened. For the record, this engine started life in 1932 as No. 9319 but between 1956 and 1959 the weight of this class was reduced and they were renumbered into the 73XX series.

*Photo: S. D. Wainwright.*

86. I'm sure we older ones can remember scenes like this, usually on a Sunday, when enthusiasts were allowed around running sheds. The smell of steam oil and coal, ashes and grime everywhere, and a strange sense of being overawed by the monsters at rest! This picture epitomizes these memories, and is of Sunderland shed in 1958. The shed man in the pit is cleaning out ashes, and behind him is one of the large 4-6-2 tanks of the old N.E. Railway. Classed as A8, they were built as 4-4-4Ts in 1963, but altered to the 4-6-2T design in 1931–36. On the right is an ex N.E.R., 0-6-0, No. 65836, Worsdell J27, having attention to its motion.

*Photo: R. Keeley.*

87. A long passenger express from Llandudno, turns into Chester hauled by a "Britannia" class 4-6-2, No. 70022 *Tornado*. The date is August 1963 and by the look of the headboards, the train has a load of returning holidaymakers. I like the double-piped water column serving two roads on the left, and the old 4 wheeled saloon coach body acting as a bike shed over on the right.

*Photo: S. D. Wainwright.*

88. There is a lot of the old L.N.E.R. atmosphere in this picture if you forget the overhead electrics, and concentrate on the "Sandringham" Class engine, and the old L.N.E.R. coaches in the bay on the right. In fact the year is 1958, the station Sheffield Victoria, and of course all the equipment is owned and operated by British Railways Eastern Region. No. 61641 *Gayton Hall* is standing at the head of the Liverpool "Boat Train" to Harwich, coast to coast in fact.

*Photo: R. Keeley.*

89. An excellent side-on portrait of a "Black 5" caught at Chester General in June 1963. The nice even lighting shows up plenty of detail in the wheels and motion of this Stanier designed engine. Small points to note include the roller bearings on the tender axles, that large rivetted balance weight on the centre drivers, the extended cab roof following the profile of the tender front, the top feed between chimney and dome, steam sanding on two wheels only etc. Two other items caught my eye, that Midland Clerestory under the bridge on the loco shed and the odd sizes in the ground disc, one large and one small.

*Photo: S. D. Wainwright.*

90. Right up to date this one, steam in the diesel electric era, alas not on the main line, but on a private company's line. The setting is Bridgnorth, the company is the Severn Valley Railway, and the engine is the preserved Class 5, *R.A.F. Biggin Hill*. What loving care has gone into this restoration. No. 45110 positively gleams, but that black smoke will not help the shiny paintwork, but perhaps there are plenty of willing hands. It's very pleasant to me, as an old Western man, to see all the interest and enthusiasm generated on the Severn Valley Railway. Notice the old G.W.R. lattice footbridge in the background, and the water column.

*Photo: Norman Preedy.*

**91.** The up Royal Scot at Acton Bridge in July 1956, with the ultimate in L.M.S. Railway locomotive design at the head. This engine, one of the largest ever to run in this country, was No. 46229 *Duchess of Hamilton*. This class of locomotive was an enlarged version of the Stanier "Princess" series and they were built at the time of the coronation of King George VI in 1937. Their purpose was to operate a new train named the "Coronation Scot", and it follows then that this class of engine should be termed the "Coronation" class. The first five were enclosed in a streamlined casing and painted Prussian blue, and several more were also streamlined but painted in the red livery. No. 46229 was one of these, as can be seen by the unusual shape of the smoke-box top. Eventually all streamlining was removed from the engines and they all became the shape seen in this picture.

*Photo: S. D. Wainwright.*

**92.** On the coast line to Holyhead close to the sea at Prestatyn, the "Irish Mail" thunders past *en route* for London with a British Railways "Britannia" in charge. Plenty of steam here! Notice the surplus roaring away from the twin safety valves. This engine was one of the several "Britannias" not to carry a name, but the number was 70049.

*Photo: S. D. Wainwright.*

**93.** In exactly the same location as that in plate 60, a majestic express sweeps past. This picture shows No. 6853 ex G.W.R. "Grange Class", *Morehampton Grange*, getting into her stride leaving Wrexham and heading south with a fully fitted (vacuum braked) freight. That is if those "C" headlamps are correct. The date was 5th August 1961.

*Photo: S. D. Wainwright.*

**94.** Another view from one of Mr. Wainwright's favourite locations but this time he has turned about face, and is looking up the gradient at Gresford towards the station. One can see that the long siding is still in place and operational at this date in 1955, as even the small siding signal is in place. Note the double arm "home" signal, because of difficulty in sighting by drivers. The coal train working "down" the bank towards Chester is being worked by a scruffy "Mogul" No. 6348, but at least she has plenty of steam in hand!

*Photo: S. D. Wainwright.*

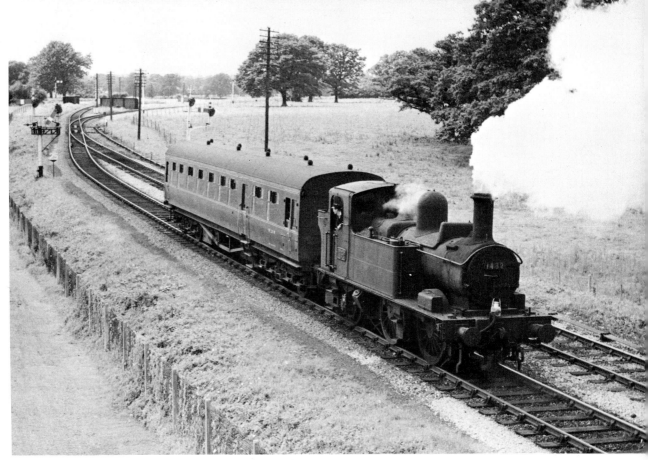

95. British Railways auto-trailer and engine. In this rural scene of Shropshire in 1962, the small 0-4-2T Collett engine is pushing one of the "A28" series of Auto-cars which were built in 1951. The actual location is Ellesmere, and this view takes in the junction straight on for Oswestry, and to the right for Wrexham, which is where this little train is routed. The little cluster of huts sited in the "V" of the junction was for housing the platelayers' mechanized trolleys.

*Photo: S. D. Wainwright.*

96. It is not often that the lineside photographer gets the chance of two trains going the same way in one picture, but it happened on this day in 1952. Just leaving Chester is the Midland 4-4-0 Compound No. 1169 designed by Fowler, heading a "Coronation Land Cruise", and in the foreground the 11.05 a.m. Chester to Oswestry is seen, in the form of another Collett 0-4-2T "1400 Class", sandwiched between two Auto-car trailers. It is just possible to see the driver in the front compartment beneath the warning bell. In this formation the engineman could operate the train from either end, the fireman remaining on the locomotive of course.

*Photo: S. D. Wainwright.*

97.   Looking down on Woodhouse station in March 1958. Situated on the old Great Central main lines from Sheffield to Retford and Nottingham, as with other G.C.R. stations, there were two platforms with goods lines at the rear of each, so making two island platforms in effect.

    Just leaving for Lincoln, is the 3.42 p.m. from Sheffield, with a Thompson 4-6-0 "B1" Class at the head, already blowing off steam. Even the strawberry and cream disguise cannot hide the lines of the first Gresley coach. How handsome they were in their original varnished teak.

*Photo: R. Keeley.*

98.   On the long straight stretch between Saltney and Pulford this little engineering Special passes by Balderton in August 1958 with No. 6320 in charge of the eight opens and two brake vans. These permanent way jobs usually took place on Sundays, when the relaying gangs could have occupation of the line for long periods for the purpose of moving track. The gang in this case can be seen sitting on the edge of the first wagon, so I presume that they were just going to dismantle some siding or other close by this actual scene.

*Photo: S. D. Wainwright.*

99.  Derbyshire in high summer of 1954. This unusual high level viewpoint dwarfs the train and reduces everything to almost model form! New Mills Central station can just be seen through the bridge at the top, with the Junction Box to the left behind the "Midland" signals. A fine piece of civil engineering here, with the high stone embankment on the left, and a steep wooded embankment on the other – a junction carved out of the hillside in fact. The engine on the local train, is one of the ex L.M.S. 0-6-0 "4F" types, designed by Fowler back in 1924.

*Photo: Norman Preedy.*

**100.** The Cambrian Coast Express from Paddington was formed on busy days, in two parts, one of which ran to Barmouth and the other to Aberystwyth, dividing their routes at Dovey Junction. In this picture we see the Barmouth portion standing at Machynlleth prior to setting off, and crossing the River Dovey at Dovey Junction, through Aberdovey, Towyn and across the Barmouth swing bridge into Barmouth itself. The date of the picture is 1959 and the engine is one of the ex-G.W.R. small 2-6-2Ts, No. 5510.

*Photo: Norman Preedy.*

101. There are two unusual features in this sunny picture of 1954 for the sharp-eyed enthusiast: firstly, the engine on the 4.30 p.m. Manchester-Llandudno Club train. This is No. 44738, one of the class "5s" which were fitted with special Caprotti valve gear, necessitating a low running plate, and consequently large splashers. There were only twenty engines so equipped, Nos. 44738-44757. Secondly, the view of Chester No. 6 box (the one on "stilts"), erected like this because of the proximity of tracks in front and behind, and the curvature of the lines.

*Photo: S. D. Wainwright.*

102. Sunderland shed again, but this time, outside in the sunshine in May 1958. As well as the saddle tank on the left, two of the massive L.N.E.R. Class "A8s" are seen being prepared. These 2 cylinder 4-6-2 tanks, started out as 4-4-4Ts but were gradually altered to the six-coupled style. This photograph does tend to remind one of what indescribably filthy places, engine sheds were towards the end of steam.

*Photo: R. Keeley.*

103. Steam everywhere, and smoke galore from the two compounds, Nos. 41100 and 41063, seen here at Stockport Edgeley in March 1958. This excursion was one of the many such spotters' specials which Ian Allan (the railway publishers) laid on for railway enthusiasts. Notice that little ground frame cabin set in between the main lines, a nice touch for a model layout!

*Photo: R. Keeley.*

104. This effective shot of No. 73117 throwing white steam against the darkening sky was taken in October of 1966 and shows the York-Bournemouth train restarting from Basingstoke on its journey to Southampton and Bournemouth. In its early days this train ran down the L.N.E.R. to Woodford, changed to Great Western metals at Banbury and then on to the Southern at Basingstoke.

*Photo: Norman Preedy.*

105. Changing from autumn to deep winter, this chill action picture of an ex G.W.R. "Hall class" No. 6996 *Blackwell Hall* was taken climbing up the gradient at Tuffley on the old joint line which runs from Standish Junction towards Gloucester. The clouds of smoke indicate that the engine is working hard, and the headlights denote the "F" code "Through Fast Freight".

*Photo: Norman Preedy.*

106. Saltney junction again and in this picture one can see the junction signal box, on the left side over the siding stop block. The train is a Leamington-Birkenhead express with a "Castle" Class No. 5063 *Earl Baldwin* at the head. The date was April 1961, and at this time genuine Great Western carriages were still in use, and two can be seen at the front of this express. One point strikes me in this photograph, where has the B.R. cast number plate from the smoke box door gone?

*Photo: S. D. Wainwright.*

107. Another look at Gresford bank and this time we see No. 2871 on an "up" freight carrying "E" headlights in August 1955. The one thing out of the ordinary about this particular shot is that large 4,000 gallon tender coupled to the 2-8-0. I presume her regular tender had developed a fault, and this "passenger" water cart was attached instead.

*Photo: S. D. Wainwright.*

108. A plume of steam bursting out of the safety valves of No. 48758 as she rolls out of Elland tunnel on the Calder Valley Line in Yorkshire. The date was 1st May 1967, and the train a Healey Mills goods. The fireman is obviously doing his best to quieten the engine, as one can see the injector being operated on the side nearest the camera. Note the headlamp dangling on the smokebox, it would appear that the proper bracket has been broken off.

*Photo: Norman Preedy.*

109. Almost fifty years separate the building dates of these two locomotives. The scene is Crewe in 1958, and No. 49229, one of the 0-8-0 ex L.N.W.R. engines built in the 1901-18 period, is pictured hauling a "dead engine" from Crewe works to the South sheds. This 2-10-0 locomotive is No. 92138, one of the "Heavy Mineral Freight" series, built for British Railways between 1954 and 1960, to a design of Mr. Riddles. These large engines were the last standard steam engines to be built in this country, and the very last one, *Evening Star*, was painted in fully lined out green livery, and turned out of Swindon Works with due ceremony and a copper topped chimney! It is astonishing to report that one of these engines working the "Flying Scotsman" was timed at 90 m.p.h.!

*Photo: S. D. Wainwright.*

110. No. 62664, *Princess Mary*, seen from the right hand side Sheffield. This engine was one of only eleven similar, which form the "D11/1" Series, known as "Enlarged Directors". How odd report that all eleven were still at work in the year of the photograph 1958, and odder still, that they should all be shedded the same depot, namely Darnall, just outside Sheffield.

*Photo: R. Keele*

**111.** On the 4th April 1958 one of the heavy 2-8-0T class of freight engines of the ex Great Western Railway is seen here at Aberbeeg in South Wales, dragging up a long line of empty coal wagons, for dispersal to the various coal pits which abound in this area. Aberbeeg was the junction, where one branch went up to Ebbw Vale and the other to Nantyglo and to a connection with Brynmawr. Railway working in the valleys was different in that the hardest haulage was in drawing the empty wagons up, the loaded vehicles coming down to Newport, Cardiff, and Barry, almost under their own momentum, the heaviest work being on the brakes.

*Photo: Norman Preedy.*

**112.** This 4-6-0 "Jubilee Class" is No. 45585, and is hauling the eight coach "The Palatine" express from Manchester towards St. Pancras London. The actual siting is Chinley South Junction, Derbyshire, and the signals show that the train is routed through Matlock to Derby and beyond. The left hand fork at this junction goes on up to Sheffield. The 3 cylinder engine's name was *Hyderabad*.

*Photo: Norman Preedy.*

**113.** One of the smallest steam engines on passenger runs in B.R. days is seen here in Somerset. No. 1463 fully lined out in British Railways green livery has just taken water at Yatton, before setting out along the branch to Clevedon. This was a push-pull service which went out with the engine leading, and returned with the trailer car running first. Note the oil-can by the smoke-box, and some enterprising shedman at Bristol has stripped the paint off the safety valve to reveal the brass.

*Photo: Norman Preedy.*

**114.** And finally this picture is of *City of Sheffield*, No. 46249, with a Glasgow-Euston express, having just left Weaver Junction and passed under the old C.L.C. line. The train is shown at Hartford on the L.N.W. mainline. This huge locomotive was one of the "Coronation" Class, a development on the "Princess Royal" series. Those built without streamlining, like this engine, had larger boilers and tenders than the original streamlining machines, and one of them, *Coronation*, No. 46220, attained a speed of 114 m.p.h. near Crewe in 1937.

*Photo: Norman Preedy.*